Dearest John

with all our love

for your

50ᵉ birthday   20ᵗʰ October 1990

from

Maggie and Michael

VISIONS OF A NOMAD

Frontispiece Bin Kabina in the western sands of the
Empty Quarter, 1948.

VISIONS
—OF A—
NOMAD

WILFRED THESIGER

COLLINS
8 GRAFTON STREET, LONDON W1
1987

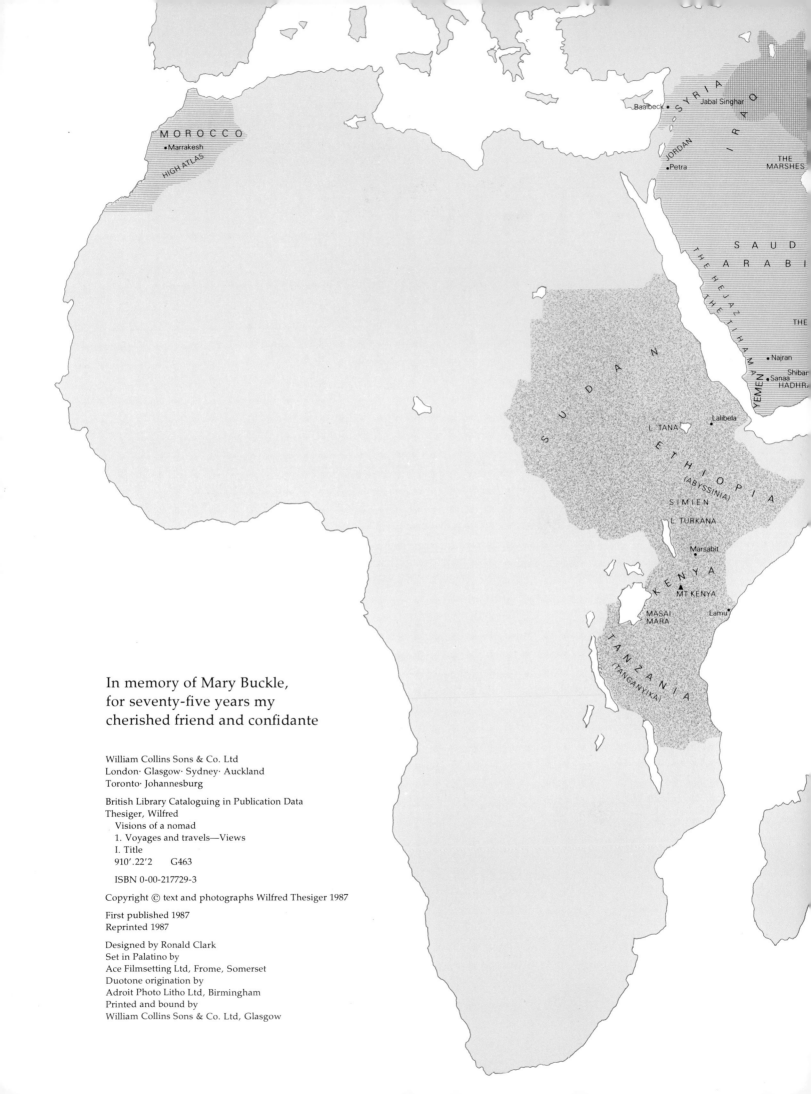

In memory of Mary Buckle,
for seventy-five years my
cherished friend and confidante

William Collins Sons & Co. Ltd
London· Glasgow· Sydney· Auckland
Toronto· Johannesburg

British Library Cataloguing in Publication Data
Thesiger, Wilfred
  Visions of a nomad
  1. Voyages and travels—Views
  I. Title
  910'.22'2   G463

  ISBN 0-00-217729-3

First published 1987
Reprinted 1987

Designed by Ronald Clark
Set in Palatino by
Ace Filmsetting Ltd, Frome, Somerset
Duotone origination by
Adroit Photo Litho Ltd, Birmingham
Printed and bound by
William Collins Sons & Co. Ltd, Glasgow

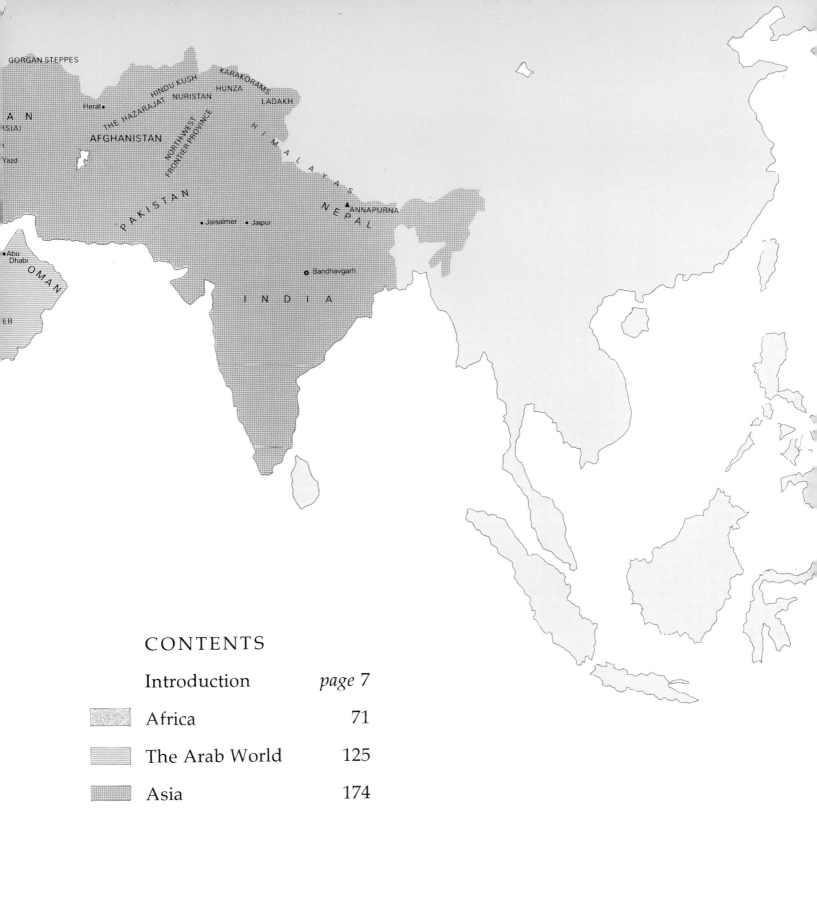

GORGAN STEPPES

KARAKORAMS

HINDU KUSH
NURISTAN HUNZA
THE HAZARAJAT LADAKH

Herat

AFGHANISTAN

Yazd

NORTHWEST
FRONTIER PROVINCE

H
I
M
A
L
A
Y
A
S

AN
(RSIA)

PAKISTAN

NEPAL

ANNAPURNA

Jaisalmer   Jaipur

Abu
Dhabi

OMAN

Bandhavgarh

ER

I N D I A

CONTENTS

Introduction   *page* 7

Africa   71

The Arab World   125

Asia   174

INTRODUCTION

I HAVE never taken any photographs with the intention of publishing them, any more than I have ever made a journey in order to write about it. I have no doubt that the early years of my life not only influenced me towards a desire for challenge and adventure but also in the choice of the places to which I travelled, and which are now the subjects of my books and my photographs.

I was born in 1910 in Ethiopia, known in those days as Abyssinia, where my father was British Minister in charge of the Legation at Addis Ababa. Ethiopia at that time was far from Europe. To get to Addis Ababa my parents had travelled by sea to Jibuti and then for a month on mules from the railhead at Dire Dawa. We remained in Ethiopia until I was nearly nine, and as a child I was captivated by the savagery and colourful pageantry of that ancient African empire, whose monarchs claimed descent from Solomon and Sheba.

The exciting and dramatic events that occurred during the revolution in 1917, which brought Haile Selassie to predominance, made an indelible impression on me. As a boy at school in England I immersed myself in tales of African hunting and adventure, determined when I grew up to spend my life among unadministered tribes in unknown lands.

My boyhood dreams were partly realized when Haile Selassie, grateful for the assistance which my father, who died in 1920, had given him during the critical days of the revolution, invited me to attend his corronation in 1930. When the spectacular ceremonies were over I spent a month on my own, hunting big game among the murderous Danakil tribes. I was only twenty at the time and this month was decisive in my life.

The reasons for my subsequent journeys have been diverse. I went to Arabia, for instance, to explore that great desert known as the Empty Quarter, but travelled to the Marshes of Iraq intending originally to shoot duck there for a fortnight. I stayed for seven years. I went to Pakistan to see Rakaposhi and other mountains in the Karakorams, to Afghanistan to travel in the barely known region of Nuristan, to Ethiopia to see the rock-hewn churches of Lalibela and other historic sites, to Tanganyika to watch the wildebeeste migration.

As I travelled I took photographs of magnificent mountain scenery, of sculptural sand dunes and of forests, of wild animals and architecture of many kinds. But by far the greatest number were of people, for it was they who afforded me the most interesting subjects. Some of them remained my companions over the years; some were with me for a month or two; others I met by chance in villages or at wells.

I was eventually induced to write *Arabian Sands* eight years after I had left Arabia, and *The Marsh Arabs* four years after I had returned from Iraq. Since then I have written *Desert, Marsh and Mountain* and *The Life of My Choice*, but I never think of myself as an author and regard my books and photographs as incidental by-products of my travels.

In selecting the photographs for this book I have been helped by Ronald Clark, Gillian Gibbins and Adrian House. We decided that the one criterion for each picture should be its quality as a photograph. We then divided them into four sections. Three of these sections comprise photographs from Africa, from the Arab world and from Asia, while the introductory section includes pictures from all three areas and is intended to illustrate my challenges and rewards both as a traveller and as a photographer.

As soon as I left Oxford in 1933 I returned to Ethiopia to explore the interior of the Danakil country. Three previous expeditions had been exterminated there by these tribesmen, who judged each other according to the number of men they had killed and castrated. By the end of a nine-month journey I had successfully penetrated and explored the fabulous Sultanate of Aussa, discovered that the Awash river terminated in a large sodium lake and had crossed the lava deserts to the coast.

On my return to England I was accepted by the Sudan Political Service and served there for five rewarding years, from 1935 to 1940, in remote areas of that vast and varied land. While I was on leave I travelled by camel from the Sudan across the Sahara to the massive volcanic mountains of Tibesti. War was declared the following year and I served in Ethiopia under Wingate when he liberated Gojjam in an astonishing campaign. I was then posted to the Middle East and fought in the Syrian campaign and with the SAS in the Western Desert.

After the war I spent five exacting but incomparable years from 1945 to 1950 with the Bedu in southern Arabia exploring the Empty Quarter, and the forbidden desert borderlands of Oman. These Bedu had no conception of a world other than their own, and when I was with them I lived and dressed as they did, anxious that nothing in their lives should be affected by my presence. All I took with me was my rifle, field glasses, compass and camera, a few books and some medicine. St John Philby, who himself crossed the Empty Quarter in 1932, told me that he always carried a radio with him on his desert journeys in order to listen to the Test matches, but I wanted no such intrusion from the outside world.

From Arabia I went to southern Iraq and lived from 1951 to 1958 with the Marsh Arabs among their reedbeds and lagoons. During the humid summer months I left the Marshes and rode with the Kurds among their mountain fastnesses, where gentians flowered among the drifts of snow.

I first went to Kenya in 1961, and with special permission travelled extensively for two years with camels in the closed Northern Provinces, on the borders of Ethiopia. Here were great herds of elephant, numerous rhino and many other wild animals, but what engrossed me were the tribesmen who ranged that arid land-scape. From my boyhood reading I was familiar with their tribal names, Samburu, Turkana, Rendile and Boran. These people still lived as they had lived in the past, unaffected as yet by the changes occurring elsewhere in a Kenya on the verge of independence. The following year I went to Tanganyika, and travelled there for six months with donkeys among the Masai.

During the next few years I accompanied the Bakhtiari in Iran on the autumn migration from the Zagros mountains to the coastal plain, and I travelled in Pakistan and Afghanistan among the Karakorams and the Hindu Kush, and in the Atlas Mountains of Morocco. I spent another two years with the Royalist forces during the civil war in the Yemen.

I returned to Kenya in 1968 and, between journeys elsewhere and sojourns in my flat in London, have lived there ever since. Much has changed in recent years. Here as elsewhere in Africa the animals have been badly poached; the rhino are now almost extinct and the elephant herds are sadly depleted.

Northern Kenya is no longer a 'closed district' and tourists in ever-increasing numbers travel around in their minibuses and converted lorries where previously the only Europeans I encountered were occasional district officers. Despite this I am always drawn back to Kenya by my affection for certain Samburu and Turkana, by the friendliness of the people as a whole, and by the unrestricted liberty of move-ment found nowhere else in Africa.

I have travelled with animals or with porters on every journey that has been of consequence to me, often in regions where no other means of transport was available. Influenced no doubt by my unusual upbringing, I have always resented cars and aeroplanes, aware even as a boy that they must inevitably diminish the world and deprive it of its fascinating diversity. Having spent years where I never even heard an engine, I flinch every time I hear a low-flying aeroplane, a passing motor bicycle, or a lorry revving up. Airports represent to me the ultimate abomina-tion, everything that I most detest in our civilization.

I realize how fortunate I am to have known Ethiopia, the Sudan, Tibesti, Iraq, Iran and Afghanistan before they were afflicted by their coups, revolutions and civil wars; above all, to have known Arabia before the development of oil transformed the country and destroyed for ever the traditional life of the desert Arabs.

Except for a few pictures of the Acropolis in Athens, I have never taken a photograph in Europe, nor photographed a European. It has never occurred to me to do so.

I started to take photographs when I attended Haile Selassie's coronation and when I hunted in the Danakil country immediately afterwards, but these early photos are just 'snaps' – evocative to me but of no artistic merit. This is a pity, for I had the opportunity to get some magnificent photographs among the Danakil, and later in the Sudan and during the war in Ethiopia, but at the time I had little care for

9

photography. I just pointed the camera and pressed the button. Only while I was in Arabia did I begin to consider the composition of each photograph, anxious to achieve the best possible result. From then on photography became a major interest.

I used an old-fashioned Kodak, belonging to my father, during my Danakil journey and took many photos. Unfortunately, something went wrong with the viewfinder and when the photos were printed I found that a strip was cut off the bottom of each one.

I bought a Leica II before going to the Sudan in 1934 and I used this camera until 1959, when I returned to Ethiopia. I possessed no additional lenses until I went to the Marshes in southern Iraq; then I bought an Elmarit/90 portrait lens and an Elmarit/35 wide-angle lens, but I still took most of my photographs with the standard lens. I changed my Leica II for a Leicaflex in 1959 and have used this camera ever since. When I went to Kenya I added an Elmarit/135 lens to my other lenses for photographing animals.

I have taken all my photographs through a yellow filter, to which I have sometimes added a polaroid filter at high altitudes. I have never used a flash, and in order to travel light have never carried a tripod. In Arabia I kept my camera in a goat-skin bag to protect it from the sand and have done so ever since. I have always used Ilford films. A month or even a year often elapsed before I could get them developed. I kept each roll in an airtight container and only in Indonesia were some of my films affected by the humidity.

I have never taken a colour photograph, nor have I ever felt the urge to do so. This may be due in part to my preference for drawings rather than paintings, my appreciation of line rather than colour. I am, however, convinced that black and white photography affords a wider and more interesting scope than colour, which by its very nature aims to reproduce exactly what is seen by the photographer. Nonetheless, until recently many of the colours were wrong and the pictures suffered in consequence. Now, because of its accuracy, colour photography lends itself ideally to animals, birds or ceremonial occasions, for example.

With black and white film, on the other hand, each subject offers its own variety of possibilities, according to the use made by the photographer of light and shade. This is particularly the case with portraits, which are my chief interest. Indeed, I believe that the majority of the photographs in this book have a quality that would have been lost in colour.

The section of photographs which follows is designed to illustrate the challenges and rewards of my travelling and photography.

As a traveller the two conditions which I desired most during any journey were remoteness (pages 14–19) and a sense of comradeship (pages 20 and 21). The region had to present a serious challenge of hardship and danger, and had if possible to be unexplored. The Danakil country and the Empty Quarter fulfilled these requirements, as to a lesser extent did Nuristan and the Karakorams. Among the inhabitants I hoped to find a comradeship with individuals that overrode differences of race, religion and culture. I found this essential comradeship among certain Bedu in Arabia, among the Marsh Arabs in Iraq and, finally, among certain tribesmen in northern Kenya.

A third condition which I particularly enjoyed was to find myself among people who knew no world other than their own (pages 22–25).

Fourth, I have always been drawn to more romantic and exciting worlds (pages 26–33), untouched by the corroding effects of our materialistic civilization. As a child I had witnessed the Shoan army return in triumph after the desperate hand-to-hand battle of Sagale only sixty miles from the Legation where we lived in Addis Ababa. In their thousands they surged past the Royal pavilion to the beat of war drums and the sound of war horns. The many chiefs were magnificent in lion's mane head-dresses and brilliant velvet cloaks, their shields and the scabbards of their great curved swords embossed with gold and silver. Horsemen charged past and there was an endless multitude on foot, brandishing swords and spears and shouting out their deeds of valour.

That day implanted in me a loathing for the drab uniformity that is spreading across the world, and gave me a lasting desire to reside among races who still retained their traditions, customs and culture. Except for southern Spain, with its Moorish past, Europe has never attracted me, either its people, its towns or its landscape, and I certainly have no wish to visit America, Australia or New Zealand.

Finally, wherever I have travelled from choice the people have worn their national or tribal dress (pages 34–39). It was always becoming, and often colourful; well suited to their mode of life, environment and climate, it never detracted from their dignity. It is unfortunate that the jacket and trousers worn by Europeans and Americans, and so widely adopted as evidence of progress, should be so unpleasing in design and so uncomfortable in hot weather. Who would choose to paint the portrait of a Lord Mayor in a lounge suit?

I have been welcomed in remote, seldom-visited regions, such as the Hazarajat or Nuristan in Afghanistan, because I was accompanied by inhabitants of those areas. Accepted by them, I was able to take photographs of these striking people, who, knowing nothing about photography, adopted no self-conscious poses; this is not easy to achieve in more sophisticated areas. When I first went to northern Kenya I took many photographs of relaxed and graceful tribesmen. Now, with the influx of tourists, all anxious to get photos, they have learnt to pose and demand money. Some, however, resent this intrusion and I have heard them protest: 'We are not wild animals to be photographed.' I have increasingly refrained from taking photographs, except from a distance, in places where I am not known and accepted. Recently I motored for a month in Rajasthan, staying each night in an hotel. I took many photographs of forts and temples, but no portraits of people.

As a photographer I have found that, apart from getting the exposure and depth of field correct, other considerations have affected the success of a photograph. For example, the exact moment caught or lost for ever (pages 40–47): a gap in clouds framing a mountain peak, a pattern of shadows on a desert landscape with a group of men and camels exactly placed, a street scene depending on the position of a moving figure, a passing canoe reflected in the water, or a leopard disturbed on its prey.

Among the landscapes (pages 48–53) which I saw as I passed slowly by – on foot, not fleetingly glimpsed from a car – I remember in particular a scene in the Karakorams with villages in a valley dwarfed by towering mountains. For me this picture symbolizes that mountain journey, and always there was the interest in seeing how a landscape could be improved by altering the foreground, sometimes by only a short distance.

The scenery of the desert, the marshes, or the mountains which I photographed will endure, but the life style of the tribesmen I was with has either changed completely, like that of the Bedu, or, as in Ethiopia, has been altered by events beyond their control.

I am glad I took so many portraits (pages 54–61), for most of them can never be repeated. They fascinate me as I look at them, reminding me vividly of my many and varied companions and of many a chance encounter. They were taken under all sorts of conditions and in a variety of light, but it was photography very different from studio portraiture. I tried to catch the turn or lift of a head, the set of the mouth, the reflection in the eyes and the combination of highlights and shadow on the face, and by so doing to get an effective picture. As with all photographs, the composition was important, the background and the set and texture of clothes. Most of my pictures are of men or boys, for I lived most of the time in a man's world, often among Muslims.

Though I know little about the technique of photography and am lost when someone discusses the workings of a camera or the processing of a film, I have an instinctive sense of composition (pages 62–65). I always try to frame a photograph so that there is no need to cut it, but this is often impossible. I realize what a help a zoom lens would have been to me.

Occasionally, and sometimes purely by chance, everything – exposure, focus, the magic moment, and the composition – coincided to produce a photograph which continues to satisfy me (pages 66–69). Over the years I have enlarged and captioned the ones which I consider the best or the most interesting.

When I browse among my sixty-five albums of these selected photographs, my most cherished possession, I live once more in a vanished world.

VISIONS OF A NOMAD

Remoteness.

Overleaf Crossing the Empty Quarter, the great
sand desert of southern Arabia.

The Chilinji Pass, 17,000 ft, on the northern frontier of Pakistan, near where Pakistan, Afghanistan, Russia and China meet.

Overleaf The Milgis Valley in northern Kenya, a closed district at the time this photograph was taken.

16

Comradeship.

Salim bin Kabina, my constant companion with bin Ghabaisha
(*above*) during the five years I was exploring in southern Arabia.

People who knew no world other than their own.

A Samburu warrior and (*below*) a Samburu married woman in northern Kenya.

Opposite An old Buddhist man, in Ladakh, northern India, near the borders of Tibet.

Above A Tigrean in northern Ethiopia.

Romantic worlds.

The Dhal Lake at Srinagar in Kashmir.

Overleaf Celebration at the Feast of the Throne in Marrakesh, 1965, with the snow-covered Atlas Mountains in the background. To me this photograph conveys all the romance of a vanished age in Morocco.

Street scene in Marrakesh, 1937, when foreign visitors were rare.

Below An ocean-going *boom* sailing home to Kuwait from Zanzibar in 1949, loaded with mangrove poles.

Opposite A picture taken during my second crossing of the Empty Quarter in 1948.

Tribal dress, always becoming and never detracting from dignity.

Below Turkana tribesmen in the closed district of northern Kenya, 1961.

Opposite A Rendile warrior near Marsabit, northern Kenya, 1961.

Below Amhara boys at Lalibela in northern Ethiopia, preparing for the priesthood, 1960.

Opposite A Boran elder in southern Ethiopia, 1959.

Opposite A Samburu family in northern Kenya.
Above Children in northern Ethiopia.

Moments caught or lost for ever.

Madan spearing fish in the Marshes of southern Iraq.

Overleaf Kandari nomads winding down towards the plains from their summer camp near Shiva Lake, the source of the Oxus in Afghanistan, 1965.

Previous page The mountain ridges at Nuristan, part of the Hindu Kush, Afghanistan, taken from the village of Mum. To me this photograph exemplifies Nuristan.

In the Masai Mara of southern Kenya. Two bull buffaloes and (*opposite*) a leopard treed by lions which had just driven it off its kill.

Landscapes.

Previous page Mount Kenya, whose glaciers remain unmelted throughout the year, although it stands on the Equator.

Left Sunset on the Marshes of southern Iraq.

Overleaf Hunza, Pakistan. The Batura glacier, a tumbled mass of boulders, stones and earth, with the underlying ice visible in only a few crevasses.

51

Portraits.

Below A Berber boy in a village in the High Atlas of Morocco.

Opposite Lawi Leboyare, the young Samburu who joined me when he was ten and who has been my companion for the past fifteen years. This photograph, taken in 1976, shows him in woman's dress, traditionally worn during the period of circumcision.

A Samburu shortly after his circumcision traditionally wearing two black ostrich feathers in a band round his forehead to which he has fastened the stuffed skins of small birds he has shot with his bow and arrows.

Opposite A Turkana warrior in northern Kenya.

Opposite Ladakhi women in northern India, north of the Himalayas.

Above An elderly Berber in a village in the High Atlas of Morocco.

A Boran elder in southern Ethiopia, 1959. Many of his tribe
emigrated into northern Kenya at the beginning of this century.

Opposite A Yazidi at Jabal Singhar in north-western Iraq. The
Yazidis are mistakenly known as devil-worshippers for their
practice of propitiating the devil.

A sense of composition.

A valley in Hunza, northern Pakistan.

Opposite A scene in the Marshes of southern Iraq.

Below Shibam, in the Hadhramaut, southern Arabia, 1947. This was the town from which I started my second crossing of the Empty Quarter.

Opposite Sanaa, capital of the Yemen, photographed in 1977, ten years after the Royalists failed to capture it during the civil war.

Photographs which satisfy me.

Below A Madan family going to market from their Marsh village. A man will always take the prow, a woman the stern.

Opposite The entrance to a *mudhif* or guest house of one of the sheikhs, built entirely of giant reeds, on dry land at the edge of the Marshes.

Opposite Bin Ghabaisha in 1946, a member of the Rashid tribe who accompanied me on my journeys in southern Arabia.

Above A Samburu warrior bathing in one of the rare streams in northern Kenya.

AFRICA

FOR ME Africa begins south of the Sahara, while North Africa belongs to the Arab world. My experience of Africa has, however, been restricted to Ethiopia, the Sudan and East Africa.

For reasons I have explained in the introduction, my Ethiopian photographs in this book date only from my return there in 1959 and 1960. In 1960 I journeyed with mules for six months through the highlands of northern Ethiopia among which the Blue Nile has its source. To the east and to the west these immense highlands end abruptly in lofty escarpments that fall to the Danakil desert and the plains of the Sudan. Much of the intervening country is cut up by deep gorges or eroded into high, sheer-sided tables, known as *ambas*. This formidable country comprises the five provinces of historic Ethiopia – Tigre, Begemder, Gojjam, Wollo and Shoa. I was familiar with southern Shoa and I had served in Gojjam during the war. I now made my way through northern Shoa, Begemder and Wollo.

I travelled on the east side of the Abbai or Blue Nile to Lake Tana, and saw the impressive Tisisat falls, below which the entire river is confined to a cleft in the basalt rock some ten feet across. From Lake Tana I went to Gondar and then to the Simien range, whose summit is among the highest mountains in Africa. By then my mules were exhausted and I lacked the time to enter Tigre. I returned by way of Lalibela, Magdala and the edge of the eastern escarpment to Addis Ababa.

The Amhara, who inhabit the provinces through which I travelled, are the dominant race in Ethiopia. Like the Tigreans, they are the descendants of the original Hamitic population with whom Semitic immigrants from southern Arabia interbred in the third and second centuries BC. Already the heirs of an ancient civilization, outdated in Africa only by Egypt, they were converted to Christianity as early as the fourth century AD.

In the fifteenth century the King of Portugal despatched a mission to Ethiopia, whose king had been identified with the mythical Prester John. The mission remained in Ethiopia for six years. Shortly after its departure Ahmad Gran invaded Ethiopia with an army recruited from the Adal and coastal tribes. Armed by the Turks with a number of muskets, they overran nearly all of Ethiopia, and the king appealed to the Portuguese for help. Christopher da Gama, the son of Vasco da Gama, with a force of Portuguese musketeers, was sent to his assistance. Christopher da Gama was killed in an early battle, Ahmad Gran in the last, and his army then disintegrated

The Portuguese may well have saved Ethiopia from absorption into the Muslim world, but now their Jesuit priests endeavoured to convert the monotheistic Ethiopian Church to Catholicism. Their activities resulted in widespread insurrection and they were eventually expelled from the country. The king then made Gondar his capital, and here he and his successors built the remarkable palace castles which still stand, and seem to me to reveal Portuguese influence.

Of all that I saw during this journey I was most impressed by the twelve rock-hewn churches at Lalibela. They ought to rank among the wonders of the world. All are below ground level. Three of them are monolithic, carved from enormous blocks of rock that had been isolated from the surrounding rock by great trenches; others, isolated on all four sides, are still attached to the rock above; while yet others are carved into the face of the rock. They were created in the eleventh century, and I was amazed at the vision that had conceived them, at the immense labour involved, especially in this sparsely inhabited area, and at the craftsmanship displayed. Each church differed completely from the others. It is now believed that they were modelled on other churches of normal construction. Very few of these model churches survived the ravages of the Muslim invasion, but I visited one such half a day's march from Lalibela.

Imrahanna Krestos stood in a large cave in the face of a cliff, surrounded by a forest of magnificent junipers and wild olives. This striking church was built of alternating layers of plaster and beams of dark, polished wood, and it looked extremely effective in the dim light of the cave. Here, as at Lalibela, I was moved by the obvious piety of the priests and by the kindness they showed me in this remote region, seldom visited by Europeans.

In the previous year I had travelled in Ethiopia south of Addis Ababa. This vast area had been conquered by Menelik, emperor from 1889 to 1910. The country bore no resemblance to northern Ethiopia. It was an extension of East Africa and the tribes I encountered were utterly distinct from their Amhara overlords. The two tribes that interested me most were the Konso and the Boran. The Konso were pagan cultivators who lived in fortified villages at five thousand feet, terraced their fields and marked their graves with effigies of the men they had killed.

The Boran were one of the largest of the Galla or Oromo tribes. They were semi-nomadic, lived in desert country near the Kenya border and owned camels, as well as cows, sheep and goats. Many of them had migrated into northern Kenya after they had been conquered by Menelik. I was to encounter them there when I went to northern Kenya two years later.

When I first went to Kenya it was still a British colony, and the Northern Frontier Province, inhabited by warlike tribes and subject to tribal raids from across the Ethiopian border, was a closed area that could be entered only with a special pass. I obtained permission to go there and for two years travelled widely with camels and a retinue of tribesmen among the Samburu, Turkana, Rendile, Gabra and Boran.

I returned to Kenya in 1968, after it had become independent, and did two more long camel journeys in the north. The two tribes with whom I became most familiar were the Samburu, an offshoot of the Masai, and the Turkana. In those days the latter were largely naked, living on both sides of Lake Turkana (previously Lake Rudolf). I have lived among these two tribes intermittently ever since.

Lawi Leboyare, a Samburu, attached himself to me when he was ten and has been my companion over the past fifteen years. He has adapted himself to his changing world, learnt to speak good English, drives a car and is a good mechanic. When he came to London to stay with me for a month, he was perfectly at home in my club and in the houses of my friends. But he is intensely proud to be a Samburu, respects his tribal customs, and, like all Samburu, sets great store by his cattle. Enterprising and responsible, he is highly thought of by both Europeans and Africans.

Samburu society, like that of many other African tribes, is organized on a system of age-sets, in which groups of contemporaries progress from boyhood.

Every fourteen years or so, the Samburu hold their circumcision and initiation ceremonies, when the boys above the age of puberty become warriors or *moran*, whose role it is to guard the cattle, water them, build them enclosures and traditionally to protect the tribe. In doing so they replace the previous age-grade, who now become elders and are free to marry. When Lawi was circumcised, I was privileged, as his honorary father, to take part in the ceremonies.

Each Samburu clan assembled its initiates, numbering sometimes a hundred or more, in specially built camps, where each of them lived with his family in a typical daub-and-wattle hut. For a fortnight or so the initiates, in traditional women's dress of tanned black goat skins, wandered round the neighbourhood in groups, and collected branches from a special tree to make bows and arrows. The evening before their circumcision their heads were shaved by their mothers and they were fitted with special skin sandals made by their sponsors. Each boy was circumcised sitting on a goat skin at the entrance to his hut while a crowd gathered round to watch. Should a boy flinch he was indelibly disgraced, and the crowd drove the family cattle from their enclosure and scattered them over the countryside.

Next day the initiated wore two black ostrich feathers in bands round their heads and from then on, until the final ceremony forty days later, shot small birds with blunted arrows and fastened their stuffed skins to their head bands. At the final ceremony each family slaughtered a cow and their sons fired off all their arrows into the distance. They then discarded their bird skins and ostrich feathers.

These initiation ceremonies are the most important event in the life of a Samburu, more so than his marriage or any other event. I remember a sophisticated Samburu government official, whose son was being initiated, saying to me, 'No one can know how important this is to us.' Yet in time they will inevitably abandon these ceremonies, as has been done by the Kikuyu.

My early journeys in northern Kenya led to my appointment as an honorary game warden. I had always been intensely interested in big game, but whereas my expeditions in Ethiopia and my years in the Sudan were spent in shooting trophies, I now only killed the occasional buck for meat and became deeply concerned with conservation. I was often on patrol in search of poachers. For a couple of interesting months I was in charge of the newly established game park on the northeast shore of Lake Turkana. This area was liable to raids by the nearby Merille tribe from Ethiopia. After one such raid I came on the corpse of a young Gabra. The Merille had excised his navel as a trophy.

For a long time I had wanted to see the great wildebeeste migration on the Serengeti plains in Tanganyika, which are a continuation of the Masai Mara on the Kenya side of the border. While in Tanganyika I spent six months travelling with donkeys among the Masai. I found it challenging getting good photographs of these people, but did not take many of the prolific game.

Having travelled so widely through the deserts and mountains, the plains and forests of Kenya, I was naturally drawn to the coast. Although I never wished to lie on the beaches, I was anxious to see the influence of the Arabs and was rewarded by the architecture and atmosphere of Mombasa and Lamu.

Opposite An Amhara in northern Ethiopia. Christian since about AD 330, they are now the dominant race.

Overleaf A view over the western escarpment north of Gondar, in northern Ethiopia, on the way to Simien, showing some of the typical flat-topped *ambas* in the background.

Opposite The great northern face of Simien, perhaps the most spectacular scene in Africa.

Above One of the palace castles at Gondar, showing, I believe, the influence of the Portuguese.

Opposite A pilgrim on his way to the rock-hewn churches of
Lalibela in northern Ethiopia.

Above Local farmers below the Simien range, seen from the east. To
the right is Ras Dashan, 15,750 ft, the fourth-highest mountain in
Africa.

Lalibela, in northern Ethiopia. A window in one of the rock-hewn churches and (*opposite*) the monolithic church of Medhane Alam, carved in one piece from the rock on which it stands.

Lalibela. Acolytes standing on a bridge over one of the trenches outside a church and (*opposite*) a *debtara*, or scribe, with a silver drum belonging to the church, beaten with other drums for the dance which follows some of the services.

Outside the church of Imrahanna Krestos concealed in a cave.
Opposite A priest at Lalibela in the doorway of one of the churches.

Below Nuns at Imraha.

Opposite The monolithic church of Emanuel at Lalibela.

89

Above Ploughing very stony ground in the highlands of northern Ethiopia.

Below Inhabitants of the shores of Lake Tana, from which the Abbai or Blue Nile flows to meet the White Nile at Khartoum.

Lake Tana. The Waito are the
only people on the lake to
build *tankwas* from bundles of
papyrus, and use them for
transport and fishing.

Overleaf Southern Ethiopia,
on the west of the Rift Valley.

Children in southern Ethiopia and (*overleaf*) their homeland.

Opposite A young Konso man in southwest Ethiopia, 1959.
Below Two women in southern Ethiopia, 1959.

Konso graves in southwest Ethiopia, marked with effigies of the dead men's victims.

Northern Kenya. Rendile watering their cattle at the deep wells of Ilaut. Standing on three tiers, men throw up leather buckets, singing a watering song as they do so.

Overleaf A group of Samburu boys a few days before their circumcision. They are wearing the traditional women's dress of black tanned goat skins for these ceremonies and are carrying sticks from which they will make bows and arrows. They discard the women's dress at the final ceremony forty days later.

Samburu boys in northern Kenya, after their circumcision. Two of them are wearing the traditional black ostrich feathers in a band round their head; all of them have the stuffed skins of small birds, which they have shot with their bows and blunted arrows, fastened to their head bands.

Young Masai in Tanganyika soon after their circumcision. They now carry bows and arrows, but still wear women's dress, which they will discard after the final ceremony.

Young Masai warriors or *moran* in Tanganyika.

Overleaf Zebra in the Masai Mara National Park. For me this photograph evokes the once-abundant wildlife of Kenya.

Marabou storks on the Uaso Nyero river in northern Kenya.

Below A cheetah in the Masai Mara.

Young Samburu *moran; (opposite)* the hair is worn in one of their distinctive styles.

Samburu *moran*, who may not marry until they become elders, approximately fourteen years after their initiation.

Opposite A Turkana married woman, carrying a gourd in which to fetch water.

Opposite An old Samburu woman with her grandchild.

Above A Turkana elder.

Overleaf A street scene in Lamu.

THE ARAB WORLD

BY 1945 when I first went to southern Arabia, the Sahara and the Libyan Desert had been explored and cars had replaced camels for any serious mapping that remained to be done. Only the Empty Quarter of southern Arabia still offered a challenging opportunity for desert exploration.

In 1929 Lawrence had written to Marshal of the Royal Air Force Sir Hugh Trenchard, suggesting that the R100 or the R101 be diverted on its trial flight to India to cross the Empty Quarter, and by so doing mark an era in exploration, since he maintained nothing but an airship could do it. Bertram Thomas, however, crossed it with camels from south to north in 1930–1, and St John Philby crossed it from the north the following year, but after that no European had even approached it until I went there in 1945. I crossed it twice with a few of the Rashid tribe and with them explored the desert borderlands of Oman. For five years I travelled with these tribesmen. Their lives were desperately hard. Hunger and thirst were their almost daily lot; they slept on the freezing sand in winter, endured in summer the intense heat in their shadeless land, always alert for raiders, with their rifles at hand.

I went there in quest of the unexplored, and I was immediately captivated by the sculptural beauty of the great dunes, the sense of endless space and the silence we have driven from our world. But it was the comradeship of my companions that drew me back there for those five years, and would have kept me there had it been possible. Without it, this harsh land would have been as meaningless to me as the Antarctic.

I was determined when I went there to live as these Bedu lived. I wanted no concessions; I was anxious to match myself against them on equal terms. They knew no world other than their own and accepted the hardships of their lives as a small price to pay for the freedom that was theirs. With the proud boast, 'We are Bedu', they met every challenge.

I saw them tested to the full, especially on our first journey across the Empty Quarter. We laboured over mountainous sand dunes, always conscious that our camels might collapse from thirst and the lack of grazing. Over the last and most difficult part of the journey it took fourteen days from one well to the next, while we rationed ourselves to a mugful of bitter-tasting water every twenty-four hours. Our food was finished by the time we reached this well and for four days we starved, while two of my companions fetched dates from the Liwa oasis. Later I was to go there, the first European to do so, but now my companions feared that my presence would cause trouble, and we still had to get back to Salala on the southern coast, travelling along the border of Oman through the territory of hostile tribesmen. This was but one of many journeys with the Rashid.

When I eventually left Arabia and parted from bin Kabina, bin Ghabaisha, bin al Kamam and the others, I knew I should never meet their like again. I had witnessed their loyalty to each other, experienced it myself, a stranger from an unknown land, evinced on several occasions at peril of their lives. I knew their pride in themselves and their tribe; their regard for the dignity of others; their hospitality when they went short to feed chance-met strangers; their generosity with money they so badly needed for their own requirements; their absolute honesty; their courage, patience and endurance and their thoughtfulness. Constant raids and counter-raids with the blood-feud dominating their existence made them careless of human life as such, but no matter how bitter a feud, torture was inconceivable.

Whether few or many, they always camped within a few feet of each other. Privacy was unknown among them; every action was seen and noted, every word registered and repeated. 'What is the news?' preceded every meeting with others. On this desert sounding-board everything that occurred, whether in the foothills of the Yemen, the borders of Oman or the Trucial Coast, was eventually known. If a man fell short by tribal standards, 'God blacken the face of so-and-so' expressed their universal condemnation.

I have encountered individuals among many races with high standards of conduct, but only among the Bedu were such standards generally observed. I was fortunate to know them before the discovery of oil in southern Arabia destroyed for ever the pattern of their lives. The years I was with them were the most memorable of my life.

During the heat of summer, when the Rashid were tied to their occasional wells, I travelled in the Hejaz mountains, anxious to see this little-known corner of Arabia. I quote this passage from *Arabian Sands* describing my first visit:

> For three months I travelled there, riding a thousand miles, partly on a camel and partly on a donkey, accompanied by a Sharifi boy from the Wadi al Ahsaba. Together we wandered through the Tihama, the hot plain that lies between the Red Sea and the mountains, passing through villages of daub-and-wattle huts reminiscent of Africa. The people here were of uncommon beauty, and pleasantly easy and informal in their manner. We watched them, dressed in loincloths and with circlets of scented herbs upon their flowing hair, dancing in the moonlight to the quickening rhythm of the drums at the annual festivals when the young men were circumcised. We stayed with the Beni Hilal, destitute descendants of the most famous of all Arab tribes, in their mat shelters in the lava fields near Birk. ... We visited weekly markets which sprang up at dawn in remote valleys in the mountains, or just for a day packed the streets of some small town. We saw towns of many sorts, Taif, Abha, Sabyia and Jizan; we climbed

126

steep passes, where baboons barked at us from the cliffs and lammergeyer sailed out over the misty depths below, and we rested beside cold streams in forests of juniper and wild olive. Sometimes we spent the night in a castle with an Amir, sometimes in a mud cabin with a slave, and everywhere we were well received. We fed well and slept in comfort, but I thought ceaselessly of the desert which I had left, remembering bin al Kamam, bin Kabina, Sultan and Musallim.

When I left southern Arabia I travelled for a while among the Kurds before visiting the Marshes in southern Iraq, where I intended to spend a fortnight shooting duck. In fact I lived there for the greater part of seven years. No European had previously lived among the Madan or Marsh Arabs, though after the First World War, while Britain administered Iraq, various officials had visited them. The Madan lived in reed houses built on small man-made islands or more often on stacked reeds just rising above the surrounding water. Their houses were full of flies and especially in warm weather there were innumerable mosquitoes. Movement in a village, even from one house to another a few yards away, was only possible in a canoe. There was nothing here to induce visits by Iraqi officials; indeed, I hardly ever met an Arab from outside the Marshes while I was among them. They did their shopping at small towns such as Majar al Kabir, on the outskirts of the Marshes, but few of them had been as far afield as Basra. The sheikhs of neighbouring tribes, to whom they owed allegiance, lived on the dry land outside the Marshes in beautifully constructed, arched houses made entirely of the giant reeds (*Phragmites communis*) brought from the Marshes by their subjects.

Falih bin Majid, one of these sheikhs, who later became a close friend, could not believe that I really intended to live among the Madan. 'Stay with me in comfort in my *mudhif*, and you can always visit the Marshes from here,' he implored me. Along the Tigris *mudhifs*, or guests houses, usually had nine to eleven arches, but on the Euphrates they comprised as many as seventeen or occasionally nineteen. The largest I saw was eighty-four feet long, eighteen feet wide and fifteen feet high. Sitting in these large *mudhifs* I always had the impression of being inside a Romanesque cathedral, an illusion enhanced by its ribbed roof and the traceried windows at either end, through which bright shafts of light came to illuminate the gloom of the interior.

In declining the sheikh's invitation to stay in his *mudhif* I explained that I had spent five years living with the Bedu and was used to discomfort. 'Among the Madan,' I said, 'I will at least have plenty of water to drink.' 'Yes,' he replied, 'you will sleep in it and be trodden on by their buffaloes.'

I had been attracted by the Marshes as soon as I saw them. Here I found an isolated and beautiful world inhabited by a people I liked on sight, who spoke an Arabic easily comprehensible to me. For thousands of years, even before the time of the Sumerians, their antecedents had lived in these Marshes as the Madan live there today. After the Arabs conquered Iraq in the seventh century, the Madan were converted to Islam, spoke Arabic and acquired the customs and ethics of the desert Arabs. I was therefore familiar with their social code and the moral values that they accepted.

Naturally they were intensely suspicious of me when I arrived among them. They hurried me from one village, fed me at midday in another and then passed me on to the next to sleep there. Gradually, however, I won a measure of acceptance; my medicine chest helped. There was no one here to tend their sick and they believed they would die if they went to a hospital. I shot the wild boars that ravaged their rice plots, and that all too often savaged and sometimes killed them while they were gathering fodder in the reedbeds for their buffaloes. This too helped me to win their confidence.

Falih bin Majid gave me a canoe such as the sheikhs used. She was a beautiful craft: thirty-six feet long, but only three and a half feet at her widest beam, her front swept forwards and upwards in a perfect curve to form a long, tapering stem, while her stern also rose in a graceful curve. Now I was joined by four lads as my permanent crew and they remained with me during the years I was in the Marshes. Accompanied by them I was welcomed in every village I visited. These Madan were a hospitable people and among them I fed well on the fish they speared, the duck I shot, rice and buffalo milk. In the evenings the smoke-filled house where I was staying would fill up with neighbours until the mat walls bulged and talented boys danced and sang in a space left for them by the coffee hearth. I felt happy among them.

While I was in the desert we had been almost continuously on the move and I rarely saw a woman, except occasionally at a well or an encampment where we spent a night. Now we moved from village to village and sometimes stayed in one or other for days on end, especially in those of my four companions. Their families, in a very real sense, became mine.

All round the widely dispersed villages were the reedbeds and lagoons of a seemingly limitless world that had never heard an engine. Here the wild geese arrived in autumn, wedge following wedge across the sky, and as they passed overhead the rise and fall of their calling evoked the far places of the earth. In winter, with the wind cold off distant snows in Luristan, the Marshes were alive with wildfowl. In the spring they were gone, but there was still a wealth of bird life, from the many eagles in the sky to the warblers among the rushes and the pelicans on the water. Then the reeds were touched with a fresh green growth and whole stretches of water were carpeted with white ranunculus or dottedwith flowering water lilies. But springtime was the prelude to the humid dust of summer and when the forty days' wind ceased in June I left to travel elsewhere.

In the summer of 1958 while I was staying with friends in Ireland I heard on the wireless that there had been a revolution in Iraq, that the Royal family had been murdered and the British Embassy had been burnt. I knew then that another chapter in my life was closed.

In 1966 and 1967 I was with the Royalist forces in the Yemen during the civil war. The Imam Badr had been overthrown in a coup in 1962 instigated by President Nasser of Egypt and the Yemen had been proclaimed a Republic. In the ensuing civil war Nasser armed and actively supported the Republicans with Egyptian troops. Until Nasser and the Russians had supplied the Yemen army with weapons it had only been armed with rifles and a few machine guns. Now the Republican forces were equipped with Ilyushin bombers, MiG fighters, artillery, armoured cars and with poison gas, which they used. The Royalists, on the other hand, were only armed with rifles, automatic weapons and four four-inch mortars, backed up by a team of French mercenaries; they were also cautiously supported by the Saudis. At first they were overwhelmed by the Republicans, who occupied most of the country, but by 1966 they had staged a comeback and by 1967 were within a few miles of Sanaa, which I expected them to capture. Dissensions among the princes lost them this opportunity.

I had always wanted to visit the Yemen, but during my travels in southern Arabia it had been forbidden and hostile territory, its desert tribes at war with the Rashid. I was therefore glad of the opportunity to see this little-known land. Prince Hasan, who commanded the forces in the north, sent me to inspect and report on one town after another that had been shattered by aerial bombing, and as a result I saw most of the country north of Sanaa, including some of the coastal plain. The following year I was with Prince Muhammad south of Sanaa; here the fighting restricted my movements.

I went back to the Yemen in 1977 and stayed with Hugh Leach in Sanaa, that ancient and spectacular Arab town, which I had so far seen only from a distance, and he motored me to other places in the Yemen I had not yet been to.

I had first seen Arabia in 1936 when I travelled back to the Sudan through Syria at the end of my leave. While I served in Syria during the war I went to Palmyra and spent a few days' leave in Jordan, where I visited Petra. After that I experienced life in the Empty Quarter and the Marshes of southern Iraq as it had existed for centuries. But now, with the changes that have occurred all over Arabia, I have no desire to return there, content just to remember Arabia as I knew it.

Overleaf In the heart of the Empty Quarter, the great sand desert of southern Arabia.

Previous page The sculptured beauty of one of the smaller dunes in the Empty Quarter. Bin Kabina is collecting plants on which to feed his camel.

Left Descending one of the big dunes in the Empty Quarter, as high as 500 ft and more.

Hawking in Abu Dhabi. One of Sheikh Zayid's falconers showing the unusual position of riding saddles in southern Arabia and (*below*) a peregrine on the hare it has just taken.

The head of a thoroughbred camel, with the traditional form of guiding rope.

Opposite A Junuba, from southern Oman.

A sheikh of the Duru. This tribe inhabited the borderlands of Oman, on the edge of the Empty Quarter. At the time of my journeys they were hostile to all Europeans and gave me serious cause for anxiety.

Opposite My two companions, bin Kabina and bin Ghabaisha, at the end of our journeys.

Bedu, at a well in the Hadhramaut, during my journey from
Salala in 1946.

Opposite A small boy of the Rashid tribe at a well in southern
Arabia.

Overleaf The ancient Hadhramauti town of Shibam.

In the Tihama or coastal plain of Arabia, between the Red Sea and the mountains, which extends from the Hejaz in the north to the Yemen in the south.

Opposite This boy of the Beni Malik, one of the tribes of the Assir in southern Hejaz, is wearing a garland of sweet-scented herbs.

Above A woman of the Assir walking home from market.

149

Previous page A group of boys at Qalat Razih, in the Yemen, soon after its capture by Royalist forces during the civil war, 1966.

Above In the Tihama of the Yemen, to which this type of head-dress is confined.

Opposite An elderly slave in the Tihama of the Assir, wearing a hat made from palm fronds.

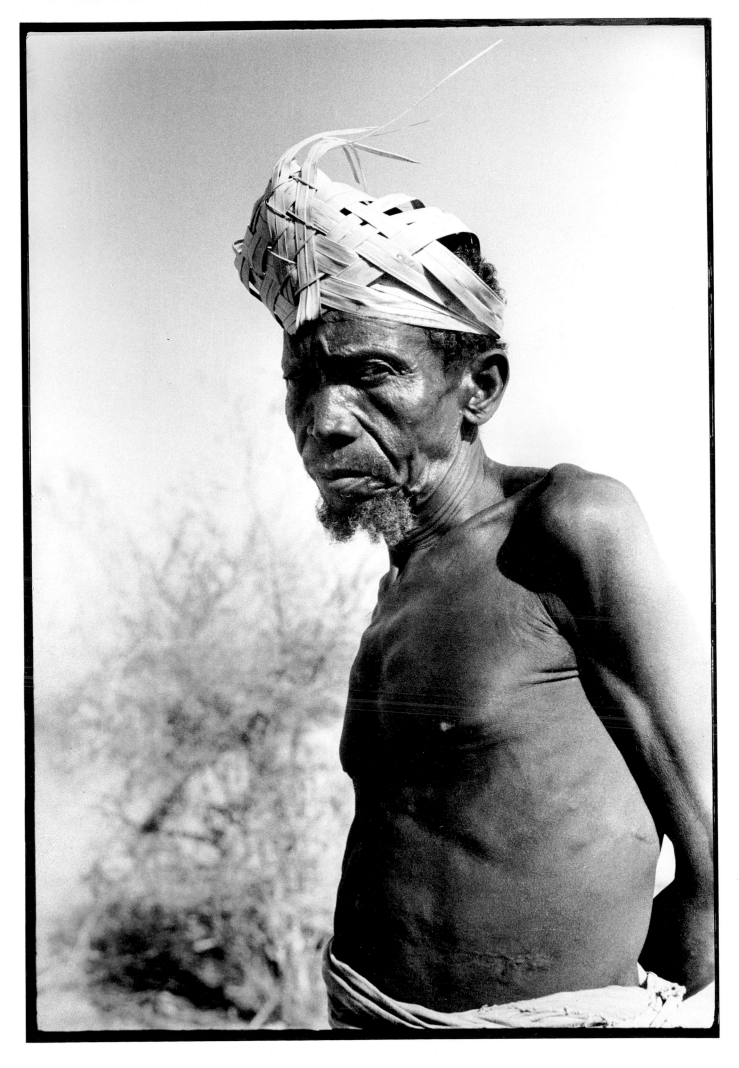

Opposite A young man in northern Yemen smoking a water pipe.

Above Young girls of the Yam tribe, near Najran in southwestern Saudi Arabia.

Opposite A boy in the Tihama of the Yemen.

Above A young Royalist soldier of the Udhr tribe in northern Yemen during the civil war.

Northern Yemen. Another young Royalist soldier of the Udhr tribe at Qaflat al Udhr.

Opposite Qaflat al Jahili after it had been bombed by the Egyptians in support of the Republicans.

Overleaf Launching a small dhow for the sheikhs to sail me round the islands on my arrival in Abu Dhabi in 1948, after my second crossing of the Empty Quarter.

The Marshes of southern Iraq, which lie on either side of the Tigris and Euphrates above their junction. Poling a canoe across shallow water and (*opposite*) a pedlar arriving at a Marsh village to buy chickens.

Overleaf A gale in the Marshes during the great floods of 1954, when large areas of desert country to the west were submerged to six feet or more.

Previous page On the Gharraf, a tributary of the Euphrates, during the floods of 1954.

Right A typical *mudhif* or guest house of a sheikh, built on dry land outside the Marshes, entirely of giant reeds. The largest I saw was 84 ft long.

Below A Marsh village with the prow of my *tarada* in the foreground: it was 36 ft long and 3 ft 6 ins at its widest beam.

Opposite The interior of a *mudhif* on the Euphrates.

Overleaf The guest tent of the sheikh of the Al Essa shepherd tribe, pitched where the desert meets the northwest edge of the central Marshes.

Below Baalbeck in the Lebanon.

Opposite My first sight of the Khazna or Treasury, as I approached Petra down the narrow gorge which leads to it, during the war. For two days I and my Arab guide were the only people there.

passes I was confronted by a succession of ranges, each crest speckled with black from the rocks showing through the snow. We scrambled down until we came to the first trees growing wherever roots could take hold, and then through forests of cedar and pine, juniper, holly oak, wild walnut and olive. At last we reached the valley bottom. From there we looked up at villages clinging to bastions of rock, thousands of feet high, each jutting house propped on stilts and seeming as small as a swallow's nest. Sometimes, following a valley, we were faced by a gorge where a weight of water hurled itself against the cliffs and our only way was up notched tree trunks placed against the polished rocks. I remember a small village called Mum. The photograph I took from there exemplifies Nuristan.

I was anxious to visit Shiva Lake in Badakhshan, in northern Afghanistan, where in summer the nomad Pathans, here known as Kandaris, congregate. We therefore crossed the Munjan Pass out of Nuristan. In Nuristan the rivers flowed to the Indus; in Badakhshan they flowed to the Oxus. We passed the ruins of a castle reputedly built by Hulagu, a grandson of Genghis Khan, and camped one night at Sar-i-Sang where lapis lazuli was still mined. All the lapis lazuli so extensively used in ancient Egypt came from this one valley in the remote mountains of Central Asia. We passed villages inhabited by Tajiks and Uzbeks and then, at a small village, turned aside across an empty plain towards a rolling sweep of bare mountains. But we were too late. Down slopes almost colourless in the hazy light but for the vagrant shadows of scattered clouds, there was winding towards us a continuous thread of men and camels. They followed no apparent course, turning, twisting and disappearing into hollows and reappearing. It was already August, and the weather had broken. The Kandaris were moving down from Shiva to the plains.

On these journeys I had passed through some of the most spectacular mountain scenery in the world and had encountered people of many different races and origins, from Mongols to Nuristanis and Pathans. They varied greatly in their customs, the clothes they wore and in the lives they led, but all were Muslims and this gave me a basic understanding of their behaviour. Though I had managed, in Peshawar and Kabul, to find someone who spoke English and was willing to accompany me, my inability to speak their language kept me apart from my porters on these journeys, and deprived me of the sense of comradeship I had known in Arabia and among the Madan in Iraq. I had felt the same handicap when I had been with the Bakhtiari on their migration in Persia, but less so when I had been with the Kurds and Yazidis in Iraq, some of whom spoke Arabic.

I went to India in 1983 and spent two months in Ladakh on the north side of the Himalayas. For me this was a totally new experience, for here I was among Buddhists and with a people akin to the Tibetans. Sir Robert ffolkes, who had been in Ladakh for five years, in charge of the Save the Children organization, had invited me to join him and he fetched me from Srinagar and motored me to Leh. He had advised me not to come before the beginning of September since the tourists, who already were overrunning Ladakh in the summer, would have left by then.

For two months we travelled with yaks or ponies from one village to the next, sometimes arriving after dark. Only in the Tibesti mountains had I seen a landscape as barren. We travelled incessantly over rocks and stones where the only vegetation was an occasional artemisia plant. We climbed high passes where a little snow still lingered, sometimes crossing two passes in a day; we skirted tremendous gorges, and at last we would reach a small village with some cultivation along a stream, perhaps bordered by tamarisk and willow. Everywhere we were welcomed, for ffolkes had done much to help these people. We stayed each night in their villages, sat round hearths in the increasing cold and drank their buttered tea. We would stay in a village for a day or two. Some of these people, especially the old women, had striking faces. I was happy to be accepted by them, able to take what photographs I wanted with no feeling of restraint.

From Ladakh I spent a month motoring through Rajasthan and visited Jaipur, where as a small boy of seven I had taken part in a tiger shoot. I saw the remote desert city of Jaisalmer and was particularly struck by the beauty of the Jain temples at Mount Abu.

While I was in India I went to the tiger sanctuary of Bandhavgarh, where I had the fascination of riding silently through the jungle on an elephant and of seeing a number of tigers. It gave me a satisfaction which I have never experienced watching lion and other animals from the confinement of a car in an African game park.

Before returning to England I spent a month in Nepal. I deliberately went there in March and April to see the rhododendrons, but for some reason they were not in flower that year. Yet although it was not a suitable season for seeing the Himalayas, which were usually shrouded in a haze, I once caught a glimpse of the Annapurna range, clearcut and beautiful after a fall of rain. This was the vision I took away with me of the Himalayas.

Northern Iraq. A young Kurdish boy and (*opposite*) a Yazidi elder in Jabal Singhar.

Opposite A young Yazidi boy in Jabal Singhar.

Below One of the domes of the eleventh-century *Masjid-i-Jumeh*, the Friday Mosque, in Isfahan, Persia.

Overleaf The *Maidan-i-Shah*, one-third of a mile long, at Isfahan. In 1949 a *doroshkeh*, or horse-drawn cab, was still a regular sight.

Previous page Part of the *Pol-i-Khaju* bridge across the Zaindeh Rud, in Isfahan, built in the seventeenth century.

Below Shepherds' tents on the southern slopes of the Elburz mountains of northern Persia; the Bakhtiari tents were very similar.

Opposite The Bakhtiari on migration in the Zagros mountains.

Opposite The site of the castle of Alamut in Persia, above the Valley of the Assassins, whose leader, the Old Man of the Mountains, captured it in AD 1090. It was eventually destroyed by a grandson of Genghis Khan.

Above Bakhtiari children.

Opposite A Turkoman on the Gorgan Steppes, near the Russian border of Persia.

Below Turkoman children in the entrance of a *yurt*, the felt-covered tent used by these people.

Opposite The Friday Mosque at Herat, western Afghanistan.

Below The mosque at Balkh, northern Afghanistan, now a village but once a city of immense antiquity.

Hazaras living west of Kabul in the Hazarajat. Their Mongol ancestors were probably left here to guard the marches of his empire by Genghis Khan's descendants.

Opposite A Ladakhi child with a baby on his back.

Above Nuristani children in the mountains of eastern Afghanistan.

Nuristanis in eastern Afghanistan. While the women cultivate the
land the men herd sheep in the mountains.

Below A Nuristani.

Opposite An old man in the Parun Valley, Nuristan.

Overleaf Northern Pakistan, near the top of the 16,000 ft Kachi Kuni Pass, on the approach to Chitral from Swat.

A Mahsud tribesman from the North-West Frontier Province of Pakistan.

Opposite A Wazir tribesman from Razmak in the North-West Frontier Province of Pakistan.

Overleaf In the Karakorams of Pakistan, north of Baltit, capital of Hunza. The picture of the villages in the valley, dwarfed by towering mountains, symbolizes this particular journey, which I undertook on the recommendation of Eric Shipton.

Ladakh, to the north of the Himalayas, adjoins Tibet. Its people are
Buddhists and akin to Tibetans.

An elderly man and woman in Ladakh.

Overleaf Our party approaching one of the high passes in Ladakh while travelling all day across this barren country.

View from the top of the monastery, near Leh in Ladakh, to the Indus and (*opposite*) the top of one of the highest passes in Ladakh, marked by a *choten*.

The sanctuary of
Bandhavgarh in central India.
This *dhole* or red dog was
photographed from the back
of an elephant.

Opposite Street scene in Jaisalmer, Rajasthan.

Below The Jain temple at Mount Abu.

Rakaposhi in the Karakorams, 25,500 ft. The great mountain dominates the valley route from Gilgit to Baltit in Hunza.

Previous page The Annapurna range, Nepal. This was the vision I took away with me of the Himalayas.